World Faiths Today Se...
Exploring Sikh...

**Who are your friends? Do you kno...
them? Do they know everything a...**

Well, this is a story about friends who do not know everything about one another. But they are starting to learn some things their friends do and why they do them. Read their story and you might learn something new too!

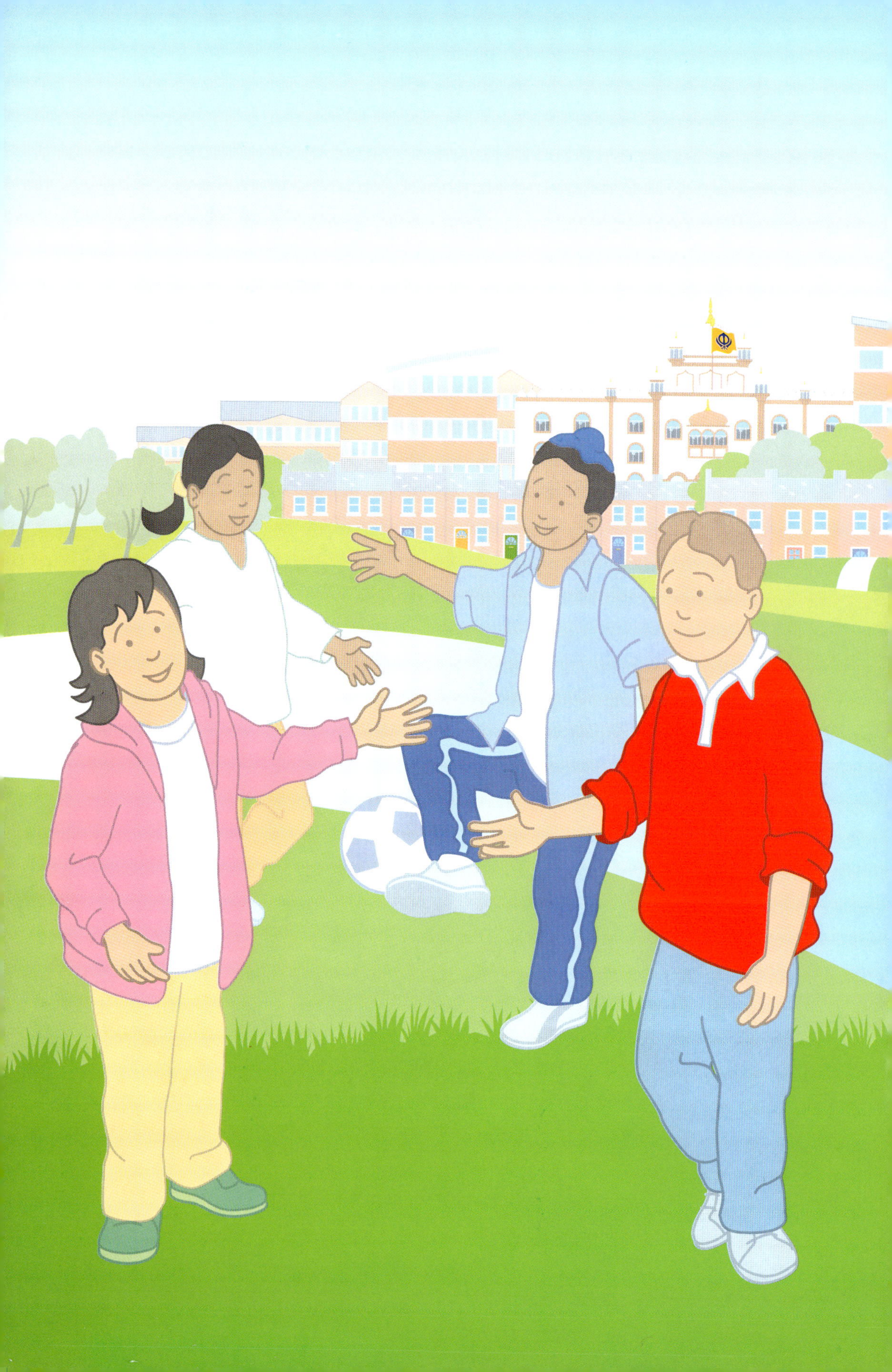

1 Visiting a gurdwara

It was the beginning of the Easter holidays and Rees and Sara had woken up early. They were staying with their favourite aunt in the city for five days, and there was so much to do. Over breakfast, Rees and Sara chatted excitedly about the phone call they had received late last night. A friend of Aunty Hafwen had called, inviting Rees and Sara to spend some time with her children, Sanjit and Yasmin.

Rees and Sara had met Sanjit and Yasmin once before, last summer at their aunt's fortieth birthday party. They had spent a wonderful afternoon playing games in the garden.

Aunty Hafwen appeared in her dressing gown. She muttered something about it being rather early.

'We are getting ready to meet Sanjit and Yasmin,' explained Sara reasonably. 'We have found the Sikh gurdwara on the map. Sanjit and Yasmin's mother said last night that I would need to borrow one of your scarves, Aunty Hafwen.'

'I think that I will wear my new blue cap,' added Rees thoughtfully.

Two long hours later, they were on their way to meet Sanjit and Yasmin.

'There it is!' cried Sara. The gurdwara was easy to recognise because it had a saffron and blue coloured flag flying outside it. Sanjit and Yasmin were waiting for them.

'Welcome to our gurdwara!' said Sanjit, smiling warmly. 'This is a very special place for our family and other Sikh families in the area. We come here to worship God together. Our name for God is Waheguru, which means Wonderful Lord.'

'A gurdwara is the guru's house,' Yasmin added. 'The guru is our teacher and our guide. The guru teaches us about Waheguru and shows us how Waheguru wants us to live. Come inside and meet our Guru!'

The foyer was busy with different colours, smells, voices, and people. The four children removed their shoes and placed them on a shoe rack by the front door.

'We need to wash our hands, and cover our heads now,' said Yasmin. 'Then we will be ready to see the Guru.'

Rees and Sara were very excited. The Guru must be very special to have a house like this. Rees put on his new blue cap and Sara wore her aunt's best red scarf.

Sanjit and Yasmin took them to a large prayer hall. In the prayer hall people were sitting on the floor. Women and girls sat together on one side and men and boys sat together on the other side.

Rees and Sara noticed that people focused their attention on a platform in front of them. On the platform sat a large book, resting on cushions and shaded by a canopy. A man read aloud from the book in the Punjabi language.

Sanjit and Yasmin approached the platform and bowed down low. They placed some apples beside other gifts of food and money.

'Where is your Guru?' whispered Sara, looking around. 'Is he that man reading from the book on the platform?'

'No,' laughed Yasmin. 'Our Guru is the book on the platform. That book is our Guru Granth Sahib. It is our teacher and our guide. I have Punjabi lessons in the gurdwara because I want to understand its teachings better.'

Musicians started playing drums and the harmonium. They encouraged those around them to sing.

'Singing hymns is one way we worship Waheguru. We call this kirtan,' explained Sanjit to Rees. 'Many of the hymns come from the Guru Granth Sahib.'

At the end of the service a sweet food called karah prashad was shared out.

'We believe that everyone is equal. Nobody is better than anyone else,' said Sanjit. 'This is why we all share karah prashad together and sit on the floor together.'

Over supper, Rees and Sara told Aunty Hafwen all about the gurdwara. Sanjit and Yasmin go to the gurdwara to worship Waheguru who is God. A gurdwara is the home of a book called the Guru Granth Sahib. The Guru Granth Sahib teaches Sanjit and Yasmin about Waheguru and how Waheguru wants them to live.

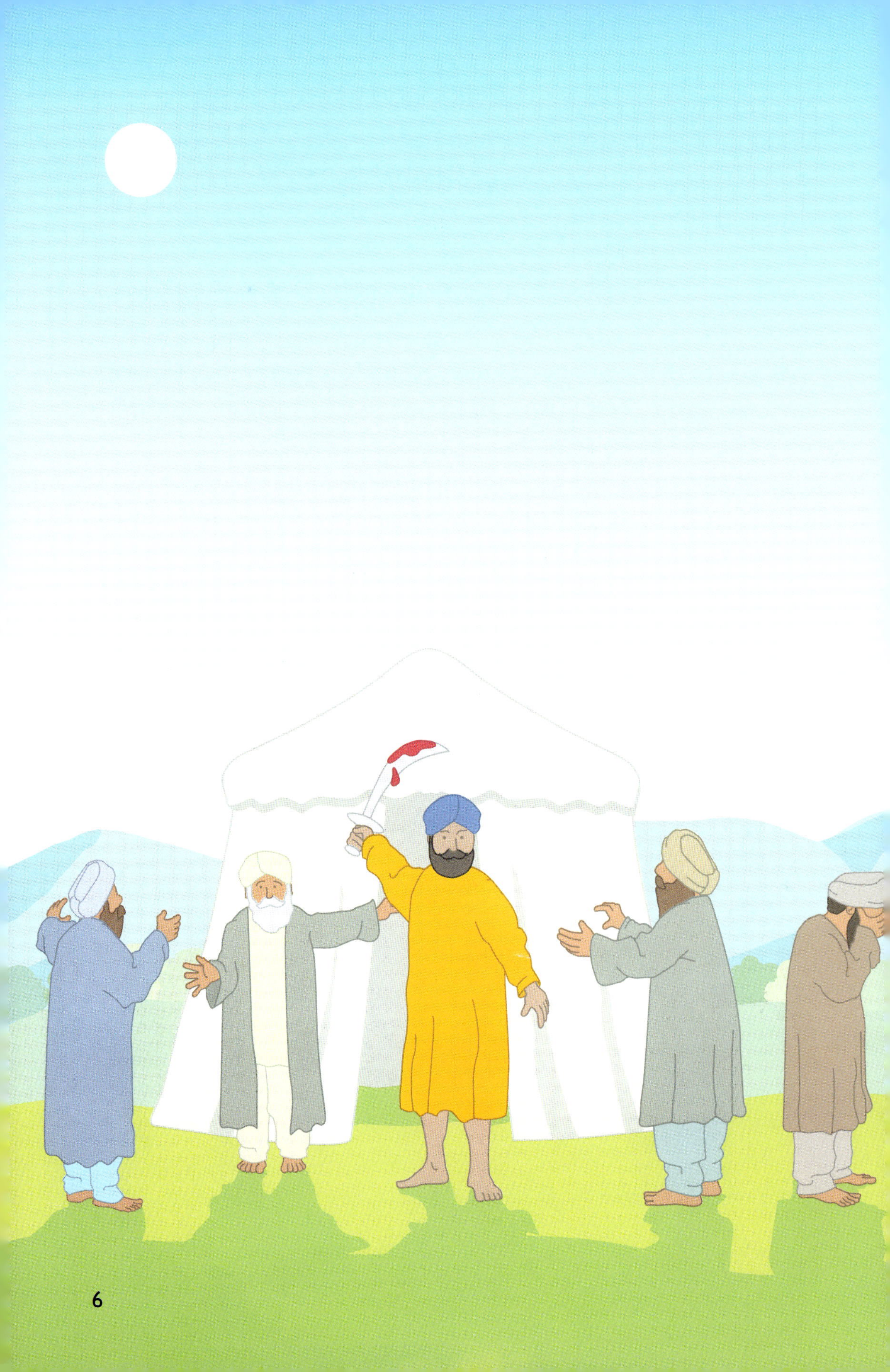

2 Celebrating Baisakhi

Rees and Sara were sitting beside their friends, Sanjit and Yasmin. Sanjit and Yasmin's grandmother had promised to read the children a Sikh story.

'Listen very carefully,' Sunita Kaur told them. 'This story will help you to understand the ceremony that you are about to see.'

It was Baisakhi Day in the year 1699. Sikhism was already 200 years old. Guru Gobind Singh stood before a large crowd of Sikhs who had gathered at Anandpur. He was dressed in a saffron-coloured tunic and a turban covered his head. His hand gripped a large sword. For over forty years many had suffered under the harsh rule of the Emperor of India. His father, Guru Tegh Bahadur, had been executed because he had protested. But, unlike his father, many people were afraid to stand up for their beliefs. The time had come for Sikhs to show courage and to defend the rights of the downtrodden – to death if that was necessary.

'Will anyone here die for me?' asked Guru Gobind Singh. 'Who will prove their faith and offer me their head?'

A frightened silence answered him. Eventually one brave Sikh stepped forward. He was taken into the tent. A few minutes later, Guru Gobind Singh came out of the tent alone. His sword dripped with blood. Exactly the same thing happened to four more Sikhs who also offered their heads.

Many Sikhs thought their Guru had gone mad and went home. The few who stayed watched with amazement as the five Sikhs walked out of the tent dressed in pure white. They were alive! These five Sikhs had proved their courage and commitment to their faith.

Guru Gobind Singh performed an amrit ceremony. This made the five Sikhs the first members of a group called the Khalsa. They would wear a special uniform so everyone would know that they were Sikhs. They would be prepared to offer their lives to defend freedom and justice for all.

Sunita Kaur closed the book and smiled at the children.

'Today, Sikhs are celebrating Baisakhi Day,' she said, 'but this is a very special Baisakhi Day for our family. Sanjit and Yasmin have an older brother called Ravi. Today, Ravi will become a member of the Khalsa. Ravi believes that he is ready to commit himself to his faith, just like those five Sikhs in 1699. Today, there are many ways to defend what we believe in apart from using the sword.'

At the ceremony Rees and Sara watched a double-edged sword stir sugar and water in a bowl to make amrit. Ravi drank some of the amrit and some of it was sprinkled over his head. He promised to commit his life to Waheguru and to follow the teachings of the Gurus. He also promised to wear the special clothes which all Khalsa Sikhs wear.

Afterwards, Ravi showed Rees and Sara his special clothes.

'I am wearing five things which start with the letter K,' explained Ravi. 'They are called the five Ks.'

Ravi showed Rees and Sara the five Ks.

'Kachera are shorts, Kara is a steel bracelet, Kirpan is a sword, Kesh is uncut hair, and Kangha is a comb,' he said. 'The five Ks remind us about what we believe in and how we ought to behave. They also help other people to recognise us as Sikhs.'

When Rees and Sara arrived back at their aunt's house, they talked about their day with Sanjit and Yasmin. On Baisakhi Day, Sikhs often choose to become members of the Khalsa. This is because the Khalsa was founded on Baisakhi day in 1699. Being a Khalsa Sikh is not easy. Khalsa Sikhs have to promise to commit their lives to Waheguru and defend what they believe in.

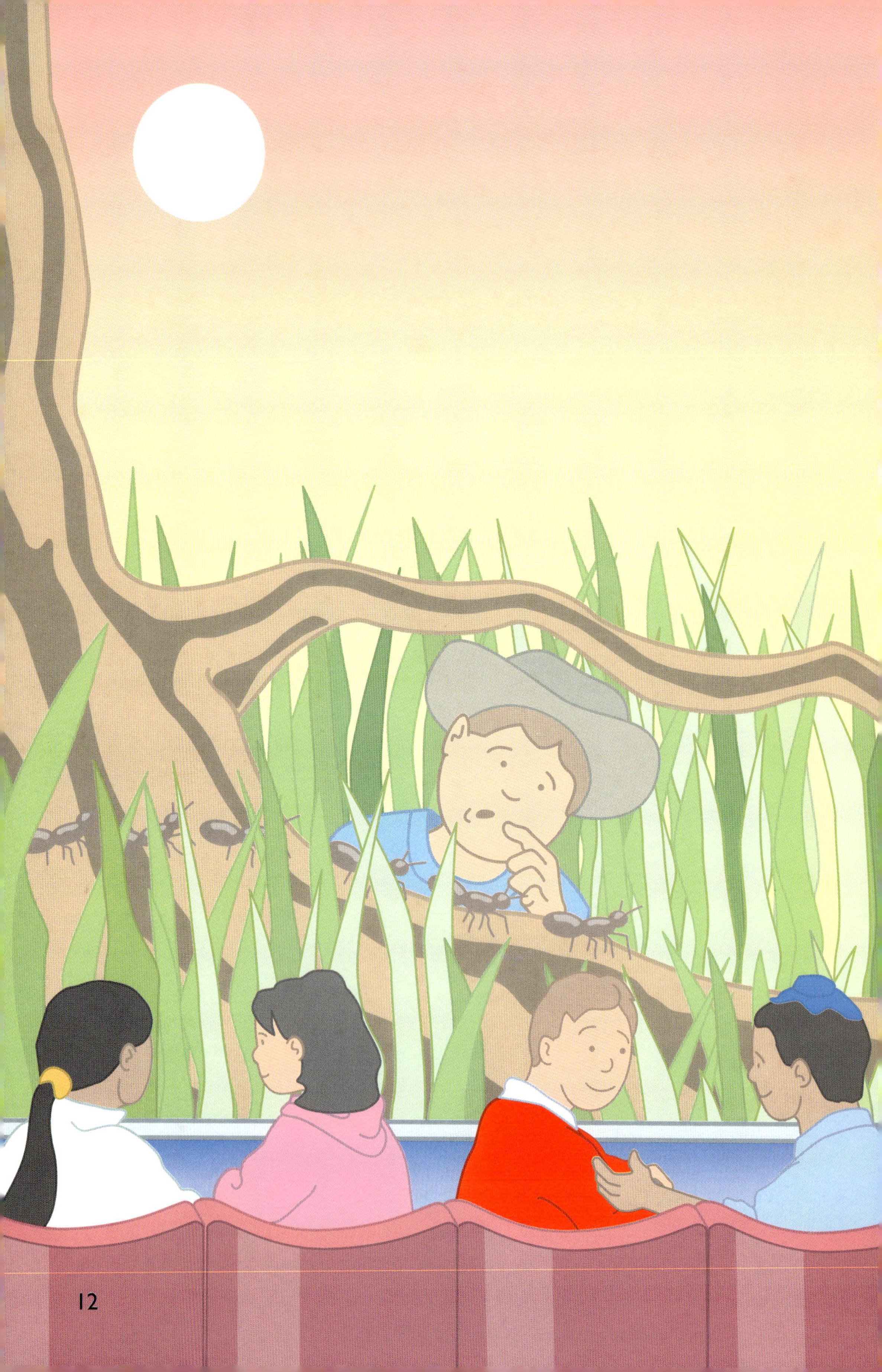

3 Leaders

It was the third day of the Easter holidays and it was raining. Aunty Hafwen suggested that Rees and Sara should watch a film with their friends, Sanjit and Yasmin.

The film they watched was about a family trek into the Australian bush. The Australian bush can be a dangerous place if you do not know what you are doing or where you are going. So the family hired a guide. The guide solemnly warned everyone to stay close together. He did not want to lose anyone in the bush.

The trek started well. The guide introduced the family to all sorts of unusual animals and plants. He seemed to know what everything was and how to find them. The trek started to go wrong when the youngest boy, Jack, forgot about the guide's warning. He was distracted by an army of ants marching along the branch of a tree. When he turned around, he was alone and lost. He did not know how to survive in the bush and did some silly and dangerous things. Eventually the guide managed to find him because he knew the area so well.

The children really enjoyed the film.

'It was lucky that the guide was so good,' said Sara, 'or otherwise Jack might never have been found!'

Sanjit agreed. 'Sikhs have guides too and these are very important to us. We call them gurus. They are a bit like the guide in the film. Gurus know where they are going and they know how to get there. They have made the journey before. God, Waheguru, has sent gurus to guide us on that same journey.'

'So where are you going? What journey is this?' asked Rees, who was both interested and confused.

'It is the most important journey of all for Sikhs. It is the journey leading us to God, Waheguru. Come home with us and I will show you some pictures of our gurus.'

At Sanjit and Yasmin's house, Rees and Sara were shown pictures of distinguished looking men.

'Since 1469, God, Waheguru, has sent ten gurus to guide us on our journey. They all came from the Punjab, in northern India. This is a picture of the first guru, Guru Nanak,' explained Yasmin. 'The gurus taught us to put God, Waheguru, at the very centre of our lives. To help us do this, we repeat Waheguru's name over and over again. We also sing hymns about Waheguru. The more we think about Waheguru, the less we think about ourselves. We become less selfish and we start to help other people. This is the journey which leads us closer to God, Waheguru.'

Sanjit rummaged around for a picture of the tenth and last guru, Guru Gobind Singh.

'Guru Gobind Singh died in 1708,' said Sanjit. 'He appointed the Guru Granth Sahib, our holy book, as our leader and our guide. It is still our holy book and guru today. It contains many of the hymns and poems of the ten gurus. You saw it when you visited the gurdwara a couple of days ago.'

'Yes, I remember,' said Sara. She pictured the book sitting comfortably on cushions. It was treated just like a human guru. 'I can see how a human guru can guide you but not a book guru,' said Sara, puzzled.

'The book contains Waheguru's word,' explained Sanjit. 'We listen to it or we read it. We think about what it means and what it teaches us. This is how Waheguru guides us.'

Later that day, Sanjit and Yasmin took Rees and Sara to see the Guru Granth Sahib in the gurdwara. They watched as a woman opened the book and read a passage from it.

'If we have a problem or simply want guidance for the day, we open the book at random. We read what it says at the top left hand page,' said Yasmin. 'In this way we discover Waheguru's will for us. We call that doing a hukam.'

Rees and Sara felt that they had learnt a lot about their new friends that afternoon. God, Waheguru, guides them through the ten gurus and a book called the Guru Granth Sahib. This helps them make the right decisions and put other people first instead of themselves. This is all part of the journey which brings them closer to God, Waheguru.

18

4 Caring for the world

Rees and Sara gazed up into blackness. There was nothing to see, just blackness, blackness, and more blackness. Suddenly there was a bright flash of light exploding outwards towards them. The universe was born. They watched with amazement as millions of galaxies were formed. In the galaxies there were millions of suns. Some suns had planets circling around them. Some planets had moons circling around them.

They saw the planet Earth circling around its own sun with the other planets. Some of these planets were enormous giants. Others were much smaller. Some were incredibly hot. Others were icy and cold. Earth was beautiful and blue with swirling clouds. As it spun like a spinning top in space, night and day were created. Whichever side faced the sun had day, while the other side had night. Everything seemed to know exactly what it should be doing.

The lights came on. The show had finished. Rees and Sara walked out of the planetarium with their friends, Sanjit and Yasmin.

'The universe is so big and I feel really small,' said Sara.

'Well, you are quite short,' said Rees, laughing. 'I want to know how it all started. How can all those things, including us, come out of blackness and nothing?'

Sanjit and Yasmin looked at each another and smiled.

'Our first teacher and guide, Guru Nanak, told us how everything began. This was over 400 years ago!' said Sanjit. 'We can read about it in our holy book, the Guru Granth Sahib. It says that the universe and everything in it was created by the will of God, Waheguru. The whole universe came from Waheguru. This makes everything very special.'

On the way home, Sanjit and Yasmin's parents stopped at a bottle and paper bank. The children helped them to put all the papers and bottles into the right banks.

'We believe that it is important to look after the world because it belongs to Waheguru,' said Yasmin. 'Recycling what we use helps to do this.'

Back at home, the children went to Sanjit's room to surf the internet. Sanjit and Yasmin wanted to show them some other things Sikhs do to look after Waheguru's world.

'We divide time into 300 year cycles,' explained Sanjit. 'For the last 300 years we were living in the cycle of the sword. A lot of bad things happened to Sikhs during that time. They had to fight to defend truth and justice. Now we are living in a new cycle. It is the cycle of creation. This means that we must look after the world Waheguru has created.'

Rees and Sara were shown pictures of Sikhs planting trees and using solar power. They saw pictures of other Sikhs trying to save water and teaching children how to look after the environment.

'It is quite easy for us to look after Waheguru's world,' said Yasmin. 'We live in a rich country. We also learn about the environment in school. But most of the world is very poor. Many poor countries cannot afford to set up projects to protect the environment. They find it hard enough just to survive. These Sikhs believe that richer countries should do what they can to help poorer countries.'

Sanjit shut down the computer. 'Follow me,' he said. 'I want you to see something in the park.'

In the park, the four children stood by the lake. It was a calm evening and the air was still. The water was like a mirror. They could see the trees and clouds reflected in it perfectly.

Sanjit picked up a small stone and threw it into the lake. They watched as circles of ripples spread outwards. The mirror was broken. The trees and the clouds disappeared.

'Did you see how the stone made one ripple, which made another ripple and then another?' asked Sanjit. 'Everything we do is like this. Everything we do affects everything else. If we recycle paper or help someone, we make good ripples. But if we forget to put litter in a bin or are unkind to someone, we make bad ripples. We may be small, but we can make a difference.'

Rees and Sara had learnt a little bit more about their friends, Sanjit and Yasmin. Sanjit and Yasmin believe that God, Waheguru, had created everything in the universe. Because of this, the world is very special and they want to look after it.

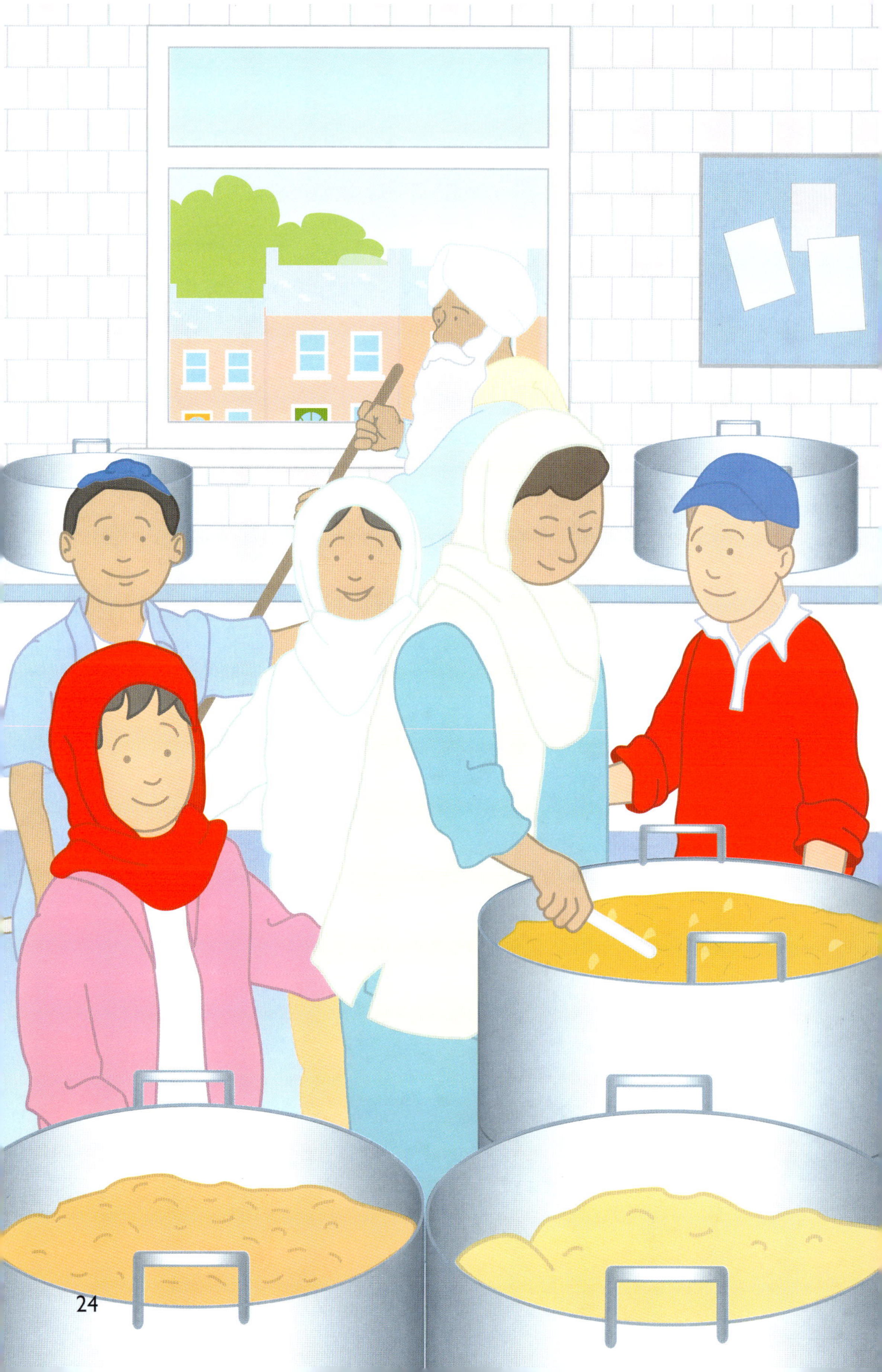

5 The Sikh kitchen

Rees and Sara were feeling sad as they packed their bags. It was the last day of their holiday with Aunty Hafwen. Soon their parents would arrive and take them home. Rees and Sara had spent most of the holiday with their friends, Sanjit and Yasmin. They would miss them. But they still had one thing to look forward to. They had arranged to meet Sanjit and Yasmin for a special lunch in their gurdwara.

Sanjit and Yasmin showed Rees and Sara around the gurdwara's enormous kitchen. Everyone was busy doing something. One woman was making chapatti bread. Another woman was slowly stirring a lentil and vegetable curry in a large pot on the stove. One man was mopping the floor. Another man was washing up.

'There are many different jobs to do in the gurdwara,' explained Yasmin. 'We all take turns in doing them. It does not matter how important you are. Everyone must practise helping and serving other people.'

'We cook only vegetarian food here because many Sikhs do not eat meat. We believe that all living things are special because God, Waheguru, has created them. For this reason, many Sikhs believe that it is wrong to harm or kill animals.'

Rees and Sara were taken to the dining room. It was full of people. They noticed that a few of them were not Sikhs.

'Anyone who is hungry can come here,' said Sanjit. 'It does not matter whether they are Sikh or not. We will give them food.'

The four children sat down at one of the long tables next to Sanjit and Yasmin's parents.

'Sitting together and eating together like this is very important for us,' explained Yasmin. 'Our religion began in India. Many people at the time were divided into different groups. Some groups thought that they were better and more important than others. They refused to sit or eat with anyone belonging to a lower group. Our first teacher and guide, Guru Nanak, said that this was not fair. No one is more important than anyone else. Everyone is equal because God, Waheguru, created them all.'

Sanjit and Yasmin's father had been listening to the conversation and nodded.

'It is not enough just to believe that everyone is equal. You have to show that you believe it in everything you do,' he said. 'This is why we sit and eat together. It is also why we take it in turns to cook, clean, and wash up in the gurdwara. God, Waheguru, wants us to serve and help other people. It does not matter who they are.'

Sara thought carefully about what Sanjit and Yasmin's father had just said.

'There is a group of girls at school who think that they are more important than anyone else,' she said. 'They all wear really nice clothes and shoes, much nicer than anyone else's. They always play together. No one else is allowed to join in.'

'It happens everywhere,' agreed Sanjit and Yasmin's father. 'It is just easier to see in India. Look at Indian names. In India a name can tell you a lot about a person. A name can tell you what kind of job a person does. You can then decide if that person is good enough for you to sit next to or to eat with. Sikhs believe that this is not fair. For that reason we give all women the same last name and the same thing happens for the men. Women are called Kaur which means "princess". Men are called Singh which means "lion". Again this shows we are all equal and no one is better than anyone else. We are all important.'

At the end of the meal, Rees and Sara cleared the table and did some washing-up. They wanted to help too.

Rees and Sara were glad that they had gone to the gurdwara for lunch. It had made them think about how people treat one another. India sounded very different from the country they lived in. But maybe people are not that different. It is easy to think that some people are better than others. Sometimes this makes people unfair and unkind.

As Rees and Sara travelled back home, they decided that they would share some of their own special things with Sanjit and Yasmin. Maybe they could do that the next holiday when they come to stay with their Aunty Hafwen again.

In the World Faiths Today Series Rees and Sara learn about the major world faiths in their own country. The seven stories in the series are:

- Exploring Islam
- Exploring Judaism
- Exploring the Parish Church
- Exploring the Orthodox Church
- Exploring Hinduism
- Exploring Buddhism
- Exploring Sikhism

Welsh National Centre for Religious Education
Bangor University
Bangor
Gwynedd
Wales

© Welsh National Centre for Religious Education, 2008.

All rights reserved. These materials are subject to copyright and may not be reproduced or published without the permission of the copyright owner.

First published 2008.

Sponsored by the Welsh Assembly Government.

British Library Cataloguing-in-Publication Data
A catalogue record for this book is available from the British Library.

ISBN 978-1-85357-186-2

Printed and bound in Wales by Gwasg Dwyfor.